SO-ALF-387

Storytime Stickers

All Kinds of Kittens

by
Kim Norman

illustrated by
Betina Ogden

STERLING and the distinctive Sterling logo are registered trademarks of
Sterling Publishing Co., Inc.

Lot#:
2 4 6 8 10 9 7 5 3 1
08/10
Published by Sterling Publishing Co., Inc.
387 Park Avenue South, New York, NY 10016
© 2010 Sterling Publishing Co., Inc.
Distributed in Canada by Sterling Publishing
c/o Canadian Manda Group, 165 Dufferin Street
Toronto, Ontario, Canada M6K 3H6
Distributed in the United Kingdom by GMC Distribution Services
Castle Place, 166 High Street, Lewes, East Sussex, England BN7 1XU
Distributed in Australia by Capricorn Link (Australia) Pty. Ltd.
P.O. Box 704, Windsor, NSW 2756, Australia

Printed in China

Sterling ISBN 978-1-4027-7464-5

For information about custom editions, special sales, premium and
corporate purchases, please contact Sterling Special Sales
Department at 800-805-5489 or specialsales@sterlingpublishing.com.

STERLING
New York / London
www.sterlingpublishing.com/kids

There are all kinds of kittens, all colors and breeds.
You'll find them wherever you go.
The mama cats teach them and see to their needs.
They wash them from whisker to toe.

Some kittens sleep indoors, in cozy warm beds,
but still they find plenty to do.
They're known to rip tissue to feathery shreds
or play hide-and-seek in a shoe.

But outdoor adventures can be just as fun,
with tree bark for sharpening claws.
Cats creep up on creatures asleep in the sun,
and beetles that dart through their paws.

Drive out to the country and go for a walk.
See barn kittens cuddled in stalls.
Then watch them go hunting and silently stalk
the mice who build nests in the walls.

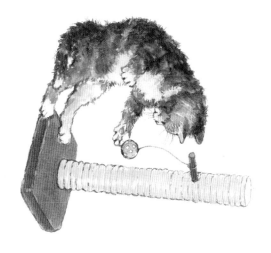

In high-rise apartments, some kittens wear bows
and live in a city of clouds.
They gaze out their windows at pigeons and crows
that swoop around taxis and crowds.

This bookshop has kittens who climb on the shelves.
A store has a lot to explore.
The kittens climb so high, they frighten themselves.
They're glad to take naps on the floor.

On boat docks, fat kittens are fishermen's pets.
They feed on the catch of the day.
Between meals, they roughhouse on crab pots and nets
and spy on the gulls in the bay.

Kittens are everywhere, morning and night,
yes, even at festivals, too.
Learn more about cats and someday you might
find just the right kitten for you!